Pollitt on Planning

**Three papers on account planning
by Stanley Pollitt**

Pollitt on Planning

**Three papers on account planning
by Stanley Pollitt**

Edited and introduced by
Paul Feldwick

With a preface by
Merry Baskin

First published 2000

Admap Publications
Farm Road, Henley-on-Thames
Oxfordshire RG9 1EJ, United Kingdom
Telephone: +44 (0) 1491 411000
Facsimile: +44 (0) 1491 571188
E-mail: admap@ntc.co.uk

A CIP catalogue record for this book is
available from the British Library

ISBN 1 84116 052 0

Typeset in 10.5/13pt Palatino by Admap Publications
Printed and bound in Great Britain by
Biddles Ltd, Guildford and King's Lynn

Contents

Preface

When Paul Feldwick first suggested to me that the Account Planning Group might co-publish a small anthology of Stanley Pollitt's papers, my first reaction was 'why?' For keen historians of the origins of account planning (and how many are there of those?) it might afford some academic interest. But for the hundreds of advertising and communications people across the world with 'planner' in their job title (doubtless spawned from Stanley and Stephen King's pioneering work 30 years ago), what possible relevance could there be? Things have changed so much since 1969, with technology and information moving at a breathtaking pace. We now find ourselves working in an ever fluid communications environment, and this could all seem much like an exercise in nostalgia.

Now, if you are asking yourself who are Stanley Pollitt and Stephen King anyway, it may be worth taking time out to give you a brief bit of background. Stanley Pollitt of BMP and Stephen King of JWT are the undisputed forefathers of account planning. In separate agencies, but at pretty much the same time, they started a revolution in the advertising world which has spread from London to other countries within advertising agencies, and from advertising agencies to direct marketing, PR, design and client research departments.

In 1964, Stephen King, dissatisfied with the workings of both the media and marketing departments in his agency, developed a new system of working (the T-Plan or Target Plan) which concentrated on combining consumer research and insights to create more effective and creative advertising. Stanley Pollitt, in 1968, concerned at the enormity of discretion given to account management in the writing of the all important creative brief, wanted a research person at the elbow of the account man. For Stanley, the voice of the consumer was of paramount importance, and using consumer research to clarify the issues and enrich the advertising development process was an essential component.

When BMP was formed, each of its three accounts was managed by an account director and an account planner. Both Stanley and Stephen shared a desire to reorganise the media, research and marketing departments, Stephen initially by a process, and Stanley via a person. Both were led towards the creation of a new department and a new discipline: the name 'account planning' was coined by Tony Stead at a JWT awayday in 1968 (and it remains one of the most obfuscatory job titles ever conceived!).

Account planning today prides itself on (still) being very hard to define. Apocryphal tale or not, a journalist from *Adweek* was recently heard asking a scion of the US branch of the Account Planning Group why was it that the definition of account planning seemed to change every year? But that's exactly the point, came the reply. Hmm.

And then I read the papers. Paul, in his introduction, has already done an excellent job of enumerating the relevant parallels between the issues and frustrations being faced then, and now by planners three decades later. Suffice to say, that if over-dependence on copy pre-testing persuasion scores, abuse of qualitative research as a semi-structured depth interview, and a shortage of decent market data, let alone anything prior to 1992, is doing your head in, you may find solace (or grist as needed) in these pages. But if you also feel that planning is losing sight of the actual core competency that we offer, herein lies a reminder.

Every planner (and everybody who values good account planning and planning craft skills) should read this little tome and give some thought to the fact that although over 30 years have passed, the planning community has multiplied and the discipline has diversified, the core beliefs actually have not changed. As long as we continue our desire to create an environment where creativity can flourish, where great ideas can be conceived, developed and embraced by client and consumer, where seeking to replace irrelevant and inappropriate research methodologies with innovative and useful ones, and where creatives and planners co-exist with an edgy tension, then here there is hope that planning can continue to make a difference. And thank you to JWT and BMP for making it possible in the first place.

Merry Baskin
Planning Director, J Walter Thompson
Chair, APG, 1998–1999

Introduction

What excuse can there be for reprinting three fugitive articles written between 20 and 30 years ago? One was written as an article for *Campaign*, the others as conference speeches that were later (fortunately) published in *Admap*. It is unlikely that any were created with an eye to posterity, and Stanley would probably not have supposed that they would still have anything to say to the advertising business on the verge of the new millennium. It is, after all, an industry that has in many ways changed enormously since the first of these pieces appeared in 1969.

Well, there are two justifications for this little book. The first, and more personal, is that 1999 was the twentieth anniversary of Stanley Pollitt's death, of a heart attack, at the untimely age of 48, and it seems as good a way as any to remember him. Nobody knows how he might have continued to influence the agency he founded, and the industry he served, had he lived, but we do know that he had already left his mark on both more powerfully than most of us are ever likely to do. In parallel with the work of his contemporaries and friends at the London office of J Walter Thompson, Stanley's legacy to advertising was a new agency structure, based on a clear philosophy, that became known as 'account planning'. This has been called the greatest innovation in agency working practice since Bill Bernbach put art directors and copywriters together in the 1950s. And account planning departments, long universal in the UK, are now increasingly common in the US and many other countries.

And yet – and here we come to the more fundamental reason for republishing these articles – after 30 years, account planning is still capable of generating heated controversy. This is not just an argument about whether it is a 'good thing' or a 'bad thing' (and there are certainly those who are actively critical) but, as with so many revolutionary movements, controversy as to what 'account planning' really means. Rival schools argue over the definition of the planner's role, the skills and experience needed for the job, the structure of a planning department and its relationship with the rest of the agency. This plurality and these debates are not necessarily a bad thing – they are, in their way, a sign of vitality. But it seems reasonable when such arguments reach a certain level to remind ourselves of what those who started the movement thought they were trying to do, and why they did it in the first place. It is in this context that Stanley's own views as he recorded them should be of interest to all those who call themselves account planners – as well as to the many other people in advertising who need to take a view on the kind of account planning, if any, that they want to work with.

Stanley Pollitt was not known as a great live presenter; mumbling, digressive, professorial, he will be remembered as often having left his audience slightly mystified. All this changed when he put pen to paper. His writing is punchy, a model of clear argument, and both his intellect and his forthright passion for his beliefs shine through. Sadly, it was all too rare that he was persuaded to write. A 'Collected Works' would not be much larger than the present volume (we know of two other papers, not without interest, but which we have chosen not to include here as being of less obvious relevance today).

This book, then, contains virtually all that we have of Stanley's own words about account planning. It is not a considered manifesto or a comprehensive exposition of an argument, but rather a series of powerful glimpses. The pieces sometimes overlap as reprinted articles commonly do.

Nevertheless a consistent, practical vision of planning as Stanley saw it does emerge from his words. The key principles of this vision, which may seem to some uncompromising today, are nevertheless worth thinking about:

- The planner is an 'expert in research' (although without the 'backroom mentality' which Stanley believed was too often found in career researchers).
- The planner uses and understands quantitative research and market data, but is not limited to numerical data, and accepts qualitative findings with equal validity and importance.
- In fact, the planner personally conducts a good deal of qualitative research, and so develops at first hand an in-depth understanding of the target audiences.
- The planner is continuously involved in the campaign, in strategic thinking, in developing the creative execution, and in assessing the results of the campaign in the market.
- To make all this possible a high ratio of account planners to account managers is needed – Stanley even recommends one-to-one.
- The planner forms part of a threesome with account manager and creative, who together share responsibility for the creation of effective advertising in a 'creative tension' – significantly, Stanley did not expect them to try to please each other too hard, but to stand up for their different points of view.

It is clear that account planning as practised today in its many variant forms differs considerably, almost everywhere, from this original vision. That is not to suggest that Stanley's way is the only way that could work – right from the start, the version of account planning introduced at J Walter Thompson was slightly different. But much of the criticism and misunderstanding of account planning derives from just those areas where current practice often differs most from the original idea – the planners who have little knowledge of, and sometimes even no apparent interest in, research; planning departments of two or three people expected to serve a medium to large agency, and who therefore, however hard they work, cannot possibly achieve the in-depth knowledge of each account that Stanley envisaged; planning relationships with creatives and account management that are either too cosy, or too remote.

What also emerges from these pages, beside the structural practicalities of planning, is a good deal of insight into the underlying philosophy behind it. Account planning grew out of a profound frustration with the ways in which research was being used in advertising agencies, but at the same time, a refusal to throw the whole idea of research out of the window (as some agencies understandably did). Stanley's anger with techniques that hindered, rather than helped, the creation of good advertising expressed itself not as an inarticulate rejection of research, but in a controlled desire to show that these techniques were theoretically weak, and their claims to be 'scientific' and objective often bogus. In their place, he fought to create a way of working where the primary purpose of research was consumer understanding, in the service of intelligent strategy and creative communication.

It would be very wrong to give the impression that Stanley fought this battle alone. In these articles he often cites others, generally from J Walter Thompson's London office, who were thinking along similar lines – Stephen King, Tom Corlett and Timothy Joyce. While Stanley was experimenting with his first planning department at Pritchard Wood, Stephen King and Tony Stead and others in what was then the Marketing Department were introducing the 'Thompson T-Plan'. In 1968, in a major reorganisation of what was then the largest agency in London, JWT merged the Marketing Department with Media Planning and Research to form the 'Account Planning' Department – Stanley himself credits JWT with the invention of the name.

In the same year, Stanley Pollitt, Martin Boase, and the whole executive board of Pritchard Wood and Partners (an Interpublic agency) resigned, after being refused a management buy-out, to start Boase Massimi Pollitt. In the new agency, account planning was an integral part of the structure from day one. From 1968, then, we can definitively date the beginning of account planning as a formal agency function. It is worth noting that in neither agency was account planning a 'bolt-on extra', nor did it represent an extra cost. In JWT it was a reorganisation of existing departments, which if anything resulted in some rationalisation of staff, although this was not the main intention; in BMP it was there from the start, and the main savings were in a smaller account management function, as it has remained ever since.

It would be equally wrong to suggest that all the battles were fought and won. Some of the techniques that Stanley found so unhelpful have returned to the UK, such as persuasion testing. More generally, research in advertising is still used far too much in place of judgment, and not nearly enough for understanding. Qualitative research continues to be too much used for the wrong reasons, and its findings undervalued. Quantitative research budgets are too often spent on copy testing and tracking studies, and not nearly enough on usage and attitude research. Market data, while it has exploded in detail and frequency, has paradoxically become harder for agencies to access and use; and when it is looked at, the focus is on short-term blips rather than understanding long-term trends. And planning departments today too often lack either the resources or the skills, or both, to counteract these tendencies.

Although there have been some positive movements – for example, the IPA Advertising Effectiveness Awards which began in 1980 – the fundamental issues in advertising have not, perhaps, changed so much from when Stanley wrote these pieces as we might have expected. The products of our industry are notoriously ephemeral – if we look at commercials from 1969 today we are likely to find them hilariously quaint and dated. The underlying debates, however, seem to change little, and if we look beneath some superficial detail, these papers are as relevant, and as controversial today as they were when they were written. I am extremely grateful to the Account Planning Group, also to BMP DDB Ltd and to NTC Publications, for their support and co-operation in making them widely available to today's audience.

Paul Feldwick
Executive Planning Director
BMP DDB Ltd

How I Started Account Planning in Agencies

Introduction

After many requests, Stanley was finally persuaded only a few weeks before he died to put on the record his own view of what he had wanted to achieve with account planning. Though fairly short and easy to read, this article (originally published in *Campaign* and reprinted with their kind permission) makes many important points, including some which still have the power to surprise us today – the claim, for example, that 'getting the advertising content right at all costs' is 'more important than agency profits, than keeping clients happy, or building an agency shop window for distinctive looking advertising'. It also roots planning firmly in the analysis of research and data, while also emphasising that the planner must be more 'practical and pragmatic' than the career researchers Stanley originally used.

PF

'Account planning' and 'account planners' have become part of agency jargon over recent years. I have been able to track down about ten agencies currently using them. There is even a new pressure group called the Account Planning Group. Unfortunately there is considerable confusion over what the terms mean, making discussion of the subject frustrating. It is worth tracing how the terms came to be introduced in 1965, how planning has evolved and what it means at BMP.

Market research in agencies has changed substantially over the past few years. Planning emerged as a particular way of dealing with this. In the 1950s, advertising agencies were the main pioneers for market research. Except for a few of the very largest advertisers, it was the advertising agency which devised total market research programmes, often from budgets in the advertising appropriation. Main agencies had either large research departments or research subsidiaries like BMRB and Research Services. It was a reflection of the broader consultancy role advertising agencies played. They were partly torch bearers for a new marketing perspective on business.

Market research in agencies has changed substantially over the past few years ... planning emerged as a particular way of dealing with this

In the sixties this changed dramatically and rapidly. More consumer goods companies were restructured along marketing lines. Included within this new 'marketing' function was a closer responsibility for market research. Companies set up their own market research departments, devised their own research programmes and commissioned research themselves. They looked to their agencies for more specialist research advice on specifically advertising matters. This again was part of a wider – and, I believe, a healthier – trend. Agencies were moving out of general consultancy and concentrating more on the professional development of ads. This meant a substantial reduction in agencies' revenue from market research – especially from commissioning major surveys. Agencies cut the numbers of market research people they had. The old research subsidiaries and some new subsidiaries formed out of separate departments became increasingly separated from their agency parents. They had to fight competitively for general research work in the open market and worked for more non-agency clients, thus losing any previous connections with and interests in advertising. A small rump of researchers stayed in the agency to cope with the *As more data relevant to sharper advertising planning were coming in, more and more people qualified to handle it were leaving the agencies* diminishing number of clients still wanting a total research service and provide some advice for other departments. This is still largely the case with most agencies today, and leaves something of a research vacuum there.

At just this time there was a considerable increase in the quality and quantity of data that was relevant to more professionally planned advertising such as company statistics, available consumer and retailer panel data and so on. Also, facilities for analysing data were becoming more sophisticated and more cheaply accessible. This posed a paradox as more data relevant to sharper advertising planning were coming in, more and more people qualified to handle it were leaving the agencies.[1]

At this point, in 1965 I found myself, essentially an account director, suddenly acquiring responsibility for research and media at the then Pritchard Wood Partners. I had a free hand to try to resolve the paradox. And this was how the idea of 'planning' and 'planners' emerged. It seemed wrong to me that it should be the account man who decided what data should be applied to ad planning and whether or not a researcher was needed. Partly because account men were rarely competent to do this – but more dangerously because as my own account man experience had shown – clients on the one hand and creative director on the other made one permanently tempted to be expedient. Too much data could be uncomfortable.

I decided therefore that a trained researcher should be put alongside the account man on every account. He should be there as of right, with equal status as a working partner.[2]

He was charged with ensuring that all the data relevant to key advertising decisions should be properly analysed, complemented with new research and brought to bear on judgments of the creative strategy and how the campaign should be appraised. Obviously all this was decided in close consultation with account man and client.

This new researcher – or account man's 'conscience' – was to be called the 'planner'. I felt existing researchers in the agency – the rump – were being misused. They were closeted in their own little back-rooms, called on at the account man's whim, dusted down and asked to express some technical view about an unfamiliar client's problem.

A trained researcher should be put alongside the account man on every account. He should be there as of right, with equal status as a working partner

PWP was not an untypical agency.[3] It had a separate media research unit where researchers were beavering away to determine how many response functions would fit on the head of a pin; a market information unit which sent market analyses through the internal post, which if read were never systematically applied to solving the main advertising problems; a general researcher, who was called in, spasmodically and inevitably superficially, to give instant advice on particular research problems; and finally a creative researcher who would occasionally be called in to conduct creative research to resolve political problems, either within the agency or between agency and client. He would usually be called in too late, when a great deal of money and personal reputations had already been committed to finished films or when the commercials were already on air.

It seemed to me that these researchers should be taken out of their back-rooms and converted to being an active part of the group involved with the central issues of advertising strategy. They were to be the new 'planners'.

This experiment proved disappointing. I found the existing agency researchers had grown cosy in their back-rooms. They did not want mainstream agency activity. They had grown too familiar with relying on techniques as a crutch, rather than thinking out more direct ways of solving problems themselves. They had grown too accustomed to being academic to know how to be practical and pragmatic. They mostly disappeared into research agencies.

Researchers should be taken out of their back-rooms and converted to being an active part of the group involved with the central issues of advertising strategy

As my first planning manager, I chose Bob Jones,[4] who had precisely the pragmatic but thorough base we wanted. We decided the only way to find this new type of researcher was to breed them ourselves from numerate but broadminded graduates. Peter Jones, first planning director at BMP, and David Cowan, our current director of planning, were the first mutations at PWP. Since then we have 'bred' from 22 trainees – 15 are still with us – and adapted five agency or company researchers – three are still with us.

That was the first phase of 'planning'. Difficult to define precisely, but it was concerned with making sure that research was a central part of the way all the main decisions were taken. Planners were people who were willing and able to take up this central role. People who were practical, pragmatic, confident and more concerned with solving problems than selling techniques.

When we set up BMP in 1968 we were already able to structure this on the account manager/account planner team basis. (JWT had adopted the planning idea in 1967 and coined the term 'account planner'. I borrowed it from them.)

From the outset at BMP we added an important new dimension to the planner's role which has almost come to be the dominant one.[5] In addition to the development of advertising strategy and campaign appraisal we started to involve planners more closely in the development of creative ideas.

It is impossible for anyone not directly brought up in advertising agencies to understand the immense importance a good agency can attach to getting the advertising content right. It can become a mission and a never-ending struggle for standards of excellence. At BMP the way we have aimed to get it right is through a sensitive balance between the most important ingredient – the intuition of talented creative people – with the experience of good account people and clients and with an early indication of consumer response which the planner is there to extract.

Traditional market researchers are heavy-handed when trying to deal with creative work

Traditional market researchers are heavy-handed when trying to deal with creative work. The nightmare world of sixties advertising when a number of now discredited mechanistic techniques were being used is a good reminder of this.[6] What we set out to do was to guide account planners to be able to be honest and clear about consumer response without stifling creativity.

All creative work – and we mean *all* creative work – at BMP is checked out qualitatively with a tightly-defined target market. Commercials are checked out in rough animatic form, typically with four discussion groups of about eight respondents each. Press advertisements are checked out in individual depth interviews with some 20 respondents. Target market samples are recruited by our own network of 80 recruiters – the majority outside London. Account planners are the moderators of the groups or depths. To give some idea of scale, we conducted some 1,200 groups last year, which arguably makes us the largest qualitative research company in the country.

This may not sound particularly unusual. To have some elements of qualitative research on rough and finished creative work is commonplace in most agencies. But I would argue that the scope and thoroughness of account planning at BMP makes it not readily – or maybe sensibly – transplantable to other agencies. It does require a particular agency environment with a number of elements present at the same time.

You can only make thoroughly professional judgments about advertising content, with some early indication of consumer response

First, it requires a total agency management commitment to getting the advertising content *right* at all costs. Getting it right being more important than maximising agency profits, more important than keeping clients happy, or building an agency shop window for distinctive-looking advertising. It means a commitment and a belief that you can only make thoroughly professional judgments about advertising content, with some early indication of consumer response. I would guess a majority of, not only creative directors, but also account directors, would find this hard to swallow. For planning to work it needs the willing acceptance of its findings by strong creative people.

John Webster[7] and his creative people have grown up with this system. John would say that 'planning' is very far from perfect – but like 'democracy' it is better than the alternatives. If advertising is to be rejected or modified it is better that this should be the result of response from the target market than the second guessing of account men or clients.

Second, it means a commitment by agency management to 'planning' absorbing an important part of agency resources. For a 'planner' to be properly effective

You need as many 'planners' as 'account men'

both in marshalling all the data relevant to advertising strategy and in carrying out the necessary qualitative research, he can only work on some three or four brands.

You need as many 'planners' as 'account men'.[8] It is interesting to compare some industry figures in this respect – in the top eight agencies billing between £35m and £65m the average number of researchers involved in advertising and creative planning is about eight. In the next 12 – billing between £15m and £30m (excluding BMP) – the average number is four. Last year, with less than £20m, we employed 18 researchers. It involves a financial commitment and the even more difficult commitment to find and train qualified people.

Third, it means changing some of the basic ground rules. Once consumer response becomes the most important element in making final advertising judgments, it makes many of the more conventional means of judgment sound hollow. You cannot combine within this same environment decisions to run advertisements because account directors or creative directors 'like' them, or because US management believes UK consumers respond in some way that the hard research evidence contradicts.

This obviously limits the territory in which the agency can operate. Evidence of consumer response can act as too much of a constraint on some clients and agency people. If it helps to limit the territory for the agency to operate in, it also helps establish a clear identity and a remarkably consistent sense of purpose within the agency. This second phase of account planning has involved it more directly in the sensitive and rightly carefully guarded area of creative ideas development.

Politically fraught, a minefield though this is, account planners at BMP seem to be coming through it well. 'Account planning' described in this way is very much a central part of the agency. As such it is not a simple task to convert to it. Although I am sure we will be hearing the terms 'account planning' and 'account planners' more widely used, I doubt whether they will carry the significance and meaning that they carry at BMP. 'Bolt-on' planning, as *Campaign* rather unkindly referred to one recent change in an agency, is not a really practical exercise.

This article originally appeared as Pollitt, S. 'How I started account planning in agencies' (1979) *Campaign*, April.

Learning from Research in the 1960s

Introduction

With this paper we go back in time ten years from the previous one. Boase Massimi Pollitt and the Planning Department at JWT are little more than one year old. But in this piece, originally given at a conference, and subsequently published in *Admap* for December 1969, Stanley only touches briefly on issues of agency structure. Here he concentrates on the ideas from which the need for a planning structure emerged, expressing both his frustration with existing advertising research, and the intellectual framework for doing things differently.

In the first part of the paper he focuses on four key themes that for him demonstrate the failings of the atomistic research approaches of the 1960s, and the need for a radically new approach. These are:

(1) Over-emphasis on recall measures in evaluating advertising.
(2) The importance of repeat purchase and the relationship between attitude and behaviour.
(3) The holistic nature of brands.
(4) The gulf between traditional researchers' models of advertising and the reality of how the best creative work actually achieves results.

What is remarkable is how each of these is still a live, and in some cases controversial, issue, 30 years later.

The paper concludes with a set of personal speculations on what the future may hold. As part of that future, we may read these with mixed feelings. Some of Stanley's ideas here may still seem revolutionary to many: that 'the rationale of creative work after it has been developed will become much more important than the initial creative brief', or the notion that creatives and planners will be more effective 'in a state of controlled friction than artificial harmony'. He also anticipates the idea of payment by results. But overall, despite many advances in the past 30 years, we might conclude that Stanley's general tone was over-optimistic.

PF

'Learning from research' is a rather impressive sounding occupation, with which I'm sure most of us want to be identified. But it is easy to be overawed by what after all is simply the business of asking people questions. For all the elaborate analysis and sophisticated processing the answers are far from sacrosanct. They can always be the wrong questions and the wrong answers, and as far as I can see they often are. What this section is about then, is how we as advertising people are able to learn to do our jobs better from such questions and answers, and the frequently obscure comments the professional question-askers tend to add to them.

Since it is obviously fashionable in the last few months of 1969 to take stock of the ten years that are just coming up, I propose to look backwards over what in very broad terms we have been able to learn from advertising research over this period, to see what use we have made of it and to make some guesses at how it may affect advertising and agencies in the future.

I have deliberately decided to omit media activities, which have usually been in the forefront of the scene. They will be exhaustively covered in the conference and already dominate the pages of *Admap*. Recognising the immense progress there has been, I sometimes wonder now whether there is not a danger of media research becoming an end in itself in introspective isolation from the rest of advertising. This seems particularly noticeable in the heroic lone grappling with response functions,[1] which some media men seem to be

We have learnt a great deal from research … ironically most of it stemming from asking the wrong people largely irrelevant questions

taking on with little or no reference to what we have learnt, sparse though it is both from creative research and the slightly more plausible models of the advertising process that are being developed.

As I hope I will be able to remind you, we have learnt a great deal from research over this relatively short period – interestingly mostly the opposite of what we set out to prove, and ironically most of it stemming from asking the wrong people largely irrelevant questions.

It was a period of unprecedented research activity into the creative, planning and media areas. It was characterised by a search to simplify, clarify and, with computers as new toys, above all quantify all those woolly, ill-defined issues which our largely innumerate predecessors had failed to grasp. In particular it was hoped to provide clearer measurable answers to such key questions as:

- How can the advertiser accurately measure the contribution his agency is making to his business?
- How can the marketing side of the agency provide more disciplined and water-tight briefs to the creative side of the agency?
- How can the creative content of advertising be evaluated and measured in a more exact way?

Specialists in advertising and creative research abounded, and we saw in fairly rapid succession a number of new theories and techniques, all aimed at putting the advertising business on a tidier, more numerical basis. In 1961 the US Association of National Advertisers put their multi-billion dollar heads together and produced *Defining Advertising Goals for Measured Advertising Results* – the late *DAGMAR*.[2] Communication was to be disentangled from sales, and the agency held responsible for it. Targets were to be set for the precise number of consumers who would be aware of a brand, would understand its sales messages, would believe in them and would take some positive action as a result. There followed a crop of advertising penetration studies, in which again there was a tally of the people aware of the products and able to recall slogans and sales points. We saw the development of pre-testing techniques in which absolute measures of 'comparative preference' resulting from the single exposures of a commercial were compared with norms of the scores from the same product groups.

We even saw the then largest international agency group citing changes in eye-pupil dilation as an alleged quantifiable predictor of the relative effectiveness of advertisements. We saw the development of 'proposition testing' so that alternative pure propositions divorced from their creative trappings could be accurately measured against each other to provide the right creative brief. Only a year ago we saw an *Admap* paper by de Vos & Peate putting forward a total measurable system of sticking numbers on unfortunate advertisements to cover every stage from their conception to their grave. We certainly saw more varied research activities questing for numbers than ever before.

In practice, variations of many of these techniques are still in use to some extent here and widely in the States. But to most of us, largely with the benefit of hindsight, they now look distinctly odd. If we are honest

Absolute measures of 'comparative preference' resulting from the single exposures of a commercial were compared with norms

enough to admit it, most of us, at the beginning of this period, would have agreed with the aims that advertising research was trying to achieve. Most of us looked at each new technique, which seemed rational and fairly respectable statistically, as something ingenious, plausible and worth a trial. There were certainly no outcries against them on a conceptual basis. I suppose there was then, as now, an uneasy feeling that if you did not agree to be measured, you must have something to hide.

It was in the practical area where they fell down, and paradoxically it was the bizarre results each research provided which prompted a more searching analysis of the data from which they stemmed. To the people trying to use the results, there was the question: if these were really the results, could we be asking the right questions of the right people? Only those who have contended with the frustration of trying to make some sense out of a proposition test can appreciate the resulting strength of the motivation to take a more fundamental look at the whole advertising process!

Our main learning from this research was negative; it was the counter measures it provoked which are likely to be the important guidelines for the future. There are four of these, which I would isolate as being of especial importance. They have all been fully written up with a depth and clarity which it would be stupid to attempt to match – I'm sure you are all only too familiar with them yourselves. A summary of their salient points might be as follows:

(1) Confirmation that 'recall' was a measurement which had little commercial significance.

For years many people in advertising, particularly creative people, have been dissatisfied with the use of 'recall' of slogans and messages as any valid measure of advertising effectiveness. Nevertheless, questions based on recall were the cornerstone of Rosser Reeves[3] and his advertising penetration theory, and it was, and still is, the basis of many pre-testing and post-testing methods. The very essence of *DAGMAR* and agency accountability rested on the ability of consumers to recall messages and slogans. Haskins[4] produced a paper in 1963 which examined some 28 case histories and concluded that there was no evidence of any positive correlation between an ability to recall messages and subsequent beliefs or actions. This included the often quoted reference to a typical case which there was of high recall for the 'Brand A costs least to buy'. (But old habits die hard and we still see many advertisers holding their agencies to account on precisely this basis. The agencies themselves are not without blame, often using 'recall' justifications where they are favourable, and knocking them down when they are not.)

Still with this impressive piece of evidence, since so many of the questions used in advertising research were previously based on recall, here was one of the first clues to account for the strange results we were finding. We had probably been asking the wrong questions.

(2) The realisation that for heavily advertised repeat purchase goods, the advertising process was not a simple model of conversion from non-use, through various stages to buying action, but a much more complex interaction between attitudes and buying behaviour.

Nearly all the previous models of the advertising process from Starch to *DAGMAR* assumed a 'common sense' sequence of moving through a number of set stages from non-use of a product to awareness, to comprehension of its sales messages, to belief in them and final buying action. The role of advertising was seen to push people one rung up the ladder nearer to the buying action. Apart from their place on the ladder all people were roughly equal. If such a model were valid it would be reasonable to expect that all the people with opportunities to see the advertising should be capable of having their attitudes significantly modified by the right advertising, thus making them more favourable prospects. A product with unfavourable attitudes associated with it was the price you paid for using a negligent agency.

A group at J Walter Thompson and the British Market Research Bureau in London, for whom Dr Timothy Joyce and Stephen King have been the most lucid spokesmen, had through their Advertising Planning Index a wealth of data which covered purchasing, attitudinal and advertising recall information over a large number of repeat purchase products. They had observed while there were consistently high positive correlations between purchasing behaviour and favourable attitudes, there was a surprisingly low connection between advertising penetration and favourable attitudes or purchasing behaviour. They were able to relate these findings to two other developments being publicised about the same time. Both Andrew Ehrenberg[5] and John Parfitt were finding in analyses of panel information that across a wide number of fields, repeat purchase patterns were remarkably stable; many users staying constant and the number of brand switchers relatively low, and new entrants lower still. Also academic work on 'Dissonance' theory[6] was highlighting people's constant struggle to keep their behaviour patterns and their attitude as closely in line as possible.

All of this suggested that it was the user rather than the new entrant that was important. Advertising's role therefore was much more one of consolidating the favourable attitudes of existing users, particularly light and medium users, with the aim of intensifying frequency of usage, than of taking the public at large through a number of apparently logical steps towards buying.

Further, favourable attitudes were so closely linked with behaviour that it became meaningless to try to relate attitude changes and advertising in any isolated way. The assessment and understanding of advertising became a much more complex analysis of changes in attitudes and brand usage over time.

As a further clue, since costs dictated that the majority of pre-testing techniques and penetration studies concentrated on general housewife samples, rather than buyers, we were not only asking the wrong questions but asking them of the wrong people.

(3) The realisation that the consumer perceives a brand and its advertising as a totality, and it is dangerous to try to measure the individual components in total isolation from one another.

The concept derived from Gestalt psychology, that consumers do not perceive a brand in parts, but as a whole, provided a further answer to some of the problems that were emerging from advertising research results. With the mood of tidiness and scientific method there was pressure to aim to isolate as many variables as possible, and subject them in lonely isolation to closely measured scrutiny. Advertising, it was argued, should be researched on a multi-stage basis. First a number of alternative 'propositions' should be measured against each other, divorced of any creative trappings. The winning proposition would then have a number of different near creative treatments, which again could be measured against each other.

Stephen King provided a masterly dissection of the absurdities inherent in the concept of separating content and treatment in a paper in the *Advertising Quarterly Review*. If you have not read it, you ought to, as it defies summary.[7]

Another clue to where we were going wrong was that many of the questions that were being asked were in a totally misleading context. But apart from these new analyses, the effect of this search for systems and measurements prompted an equally significant reaction from within the agency business itself, something we might call:

(4) The creative backlash

There has always been an important element of independent creative thinking in advertising; obviously this was how it ever got off the ground. But at this particular time we saw the emergence of a new wave of creative thinking, particularly in the States, but also with significant people throughout Europe.

The concept derived from Gestalt psychology, that consumers do not perceive a brand in parts, but as a whole

In a way it was a creative wave, which was stronger, more confident, and with people like Bill Bernbach[8] certainly more articulate than anything that had preceded it.

Bernbach was a spokesman for a new type of agency creative man, born and bred in advertising, with nothing in common with the frustrated 'graphos' and 'lits' of the past. They saw themselves as professional communicators, and as such were equally bewildered with much of the folklore of advertising techniques, built on the same shaky foundations as the methods of advertising research we have just been discussing. They questioned the style of advertising, which seemed to underestimate the increasingly intelligent audience at which it was directed. They also questioned the dullness and irritation of so much of the current advertising they saw, which had largely arisen from a desire to produce the right results on what were seen, as we know naively, as the all-important 'recall' scores.

They recognised communications as a two-way operation, not as a one-sided proclamation to dumb innocents waiting to be herded one rung up the theoretical ladder towards a sale. They had their own version of 'Reality in Advertising', which was virtually the opposite of the original Rosser Reeves edition. Their real advertising world was a place where it was necessary to start from the product and be simple, direct, essentially honest and credible and emerge as a sponsoring salesman who was informed, likeable and reasonable. They flouted many of the holy cows of advertising in particular spheres and with such campaigns as Volkswagen and Alka Seltzer, managed in many instances to flout them successfully.

The existence of this type of thinking and the growth and success of agencies with such philosophies, at precisely the time when a more systematic approach to marketing communications was in such serious difficulties, with unworkable results emerging from its research, was obviously an important issue on the sidelines. If nothing else it suggested that it could be safe to drop some of the inhibitions that beset marketing management in its search for measured results.

Bernbach was a spokesman for a new type of agency creative man ... they questioned the style of advertising, which seemed to underestimate the increasingly intelligent audience at which it was directed

These were the advertising research activities, with all their mistakes and the pressures to make them workable which we saw in the 1960s. The extent to which they were wrongly aimed, trying to provide answers to questions we are nowhere near ready to ask, is probably controversial. Still I do not think there will be much argument about the disappointment we have all experienced in the results. As I suggested at the outset, we have learnt, or certainly ought to have learnt, a great deal. Full of personal bias, I would like to make a number of guesses as to how the lessons we ought to have learnt are likely to affect advertising and agencies over the next few years. These would be the sort of guesses I would make:

- There will be a greater awareness of the complexity of the advertising process. This may mean that we will be less impatient to search for apparently simple numerical measurements of individual parts of it. The largely innumerate people concerned with applying advertising research results will be rather more disillusioned and sceptical of numbers than they have been in the past. To them the absurdities and inconsistencies of verbal arguments are things with which they can cope far more easily than numbers. A simple fact which the numerate people who predominate in advertising research never seem to grasp, is that numbers to the innumerate are seen as infallible. Liberally used as they have been in advertising research in the 1960s, they have come to be associated with wrong and impractical findings, as such they are something of a God that has failed.

Numbers to the innumerate are seen as infallible

- New techniques offering simple solutions to advertising problems will be viewed with greater scepticism and suspicion. Because of a greater realisation of the complexity of the process, emphasis is likely to shift from detailed examination of the parts to more effort being applied to measure the effects of *total* campaigns. Inevitably this will lead to an analysis of the relationship between advertising, purchasing behaviour and attitudes. It may be that this will not provide straightforward answers, but significant changes of advertising strategy are likely to produce clearly detectable effects on attitudes and behaviour over reasonable time spans (six to twelve months). Almost certainly there will be more experimentation in this area. We are likely to learn more from this than previous efforts.

- While we are closer to some understanding of how advertising works in repeat purchase fields, there are many product areas with high advertising expenditures, where the process is even more confused. We are likely to see more effort on basic groundwork to produce better hypothetical models to fit these markets and, until these are available, our experience from repeat purchase fields suggests expenditure on most advertising research is likely to be wasted.

- The greater attention to viewing advertising as a totality rather than a fruitless scrutiny of its components, is likely to call for a new breed of advertising researcher. The contribution of the relatively low narrow specialisations of media research, creative research, or market research within the agency, are likely to be less highly valued. The 'Planner', a man with research training, equally at home with all aspects of advertising research and capable of an intelligent co-ordination of all data relevant to a client's advertising problems will be someone of growing importance to agencies and advertisers. This will call for a redefinition of the media planning function in agencies.

- The advertiser's emphasis on the creative contribution an agency can make is already apparent and will increase in importance. In agency organisation terms, this will mean coming to grips with the need to accommodate the intuitive contribution he has to make. It will mean putting an equal value on creative insights, as on the logical step-by-step approach of the planner and marketing man. It will mean that the whole process of

The rationale of creative work after it has been developed, will become much more important than the initial creative brief creative exploration will become more important in specifying the nature of the creative work, than the attempted watertight creative briefs of the past. The rationale of creative work after it has been developed, will become much more important than the initial creative brief.

- Pre-testing of advertising is likely to become more qualitative in nature, and to be more concerned with comprehension and the qualitative aspects of consumer 'involvement' than to attempt to provide any absolute measures. Inevitably some advertisers will resist their loss of the convenient old yardsticks and absolute measurements provided, but they will find themselves in an increasingly untenable rational position.

The creative man, the new type of 'planner' and the account man ... are likely to work together more in a state of controlled friction than artificial harmony

- The creative man, the new type of 'planner' and the account man in a new role as essentially a businessman with a flair for advertising, are all likely to have greater equality of status. And all of them are likely to be directly involved with the client. Because of their different mental processes and ways of tackling problems they are likely to work together more in a state of controlled friction than artificial harmony. Agency management will be the arbiter for final recommendations.
- The so-called 'Marketing' agencies will come under greater pressure. Built on particular systems and disciplines in which the purely step-by-step reasoning has predominated, the fact as we have seen that such systems have been largely based on asking the wrong people the

wrong questions in the wrong context may not pass entirely unnoticed. Indeed some advertisers may look at these agency emperors of the 1960s and not be afraid now to notice that they have no clothes.

- Deprived of many of the ready-made measurements with which to evaluate agency performance, the agency/client relationship may undergo some changes. The advertiser will be able to decide more arbitrarily and openly whether the particular agency group with whom they work is making a genuine creative contribution to most aspects of their marketing operation. Like the client, marketing people themselves are bound to be judged by sales and profit results over time. Some of the previously artificial methods of agency accountability are likely to be outdated.

Maybe all this will turn out to be mere wishful thinking and that advertising people will persist in trying to quantify the unquantifiable, clients will persist in assessing their agencies on artificial measurements and agencies continue to produce ready-made total systems which stifle the intuitive contribution of their best creative people. If this is so it will be a pity because it will mean we will have learnt very little from the advertising research of the 1960s.

This article originally appeared as Pollitt, S. 'Learning from research in the 'sixties' (1969) *Admap*, December.

Has Anything Gone Wrong with Advertising Research?

Introduction

This paper, presented at a Media Research Group conference some 18 months after 'Learning from research in the 1960s', to some extent revisits the same ground, but also offers some new perspectives.

Once again, Stanley is critical of hierarchical models of advertising effect, and cites the work of Ehrenberg, King and Joyce to justify an alternative set of theories. But here he goes on to make an even more explicit statement of his own position. Rejecting both the proposition that 'advertising is such a complex process that it defies researching' and that 'everything is capable of quantification', he spells out a third way: 'We must form the best informed judgement that we can from the most detailed analysis of quantified hard data, but should feel confident in using soft data as well.' To get the right balance between data and insight requires a new breed of advertising professional: the account planner.

PF

The rather odd subject of the paper I was given on which to speak certainly provides plenty of scope. Advertising research is probably the area richest in failure in the whole market research field. Put at its crudest, none of the existing techniques for *quantifying* the potential effectiveness of individual advertisements or the specific contribution advertising makes to campaigns has provided any relevant or seriously usable data. The dimensions of the problem are much larger than we often imply. We are not dealing with something which is at present just a little bit imperfect, or with existing techniques not working *partially*, but of their not working at all.

While we may well all agree about the failure, I am sure there will be quite a lot of disagreement on the reasons why techniques seeking to quantify advertising response have not worked, and even more on what we should be doing to improve the basis for decisions about advertising in the future. Let me try to put forward one point of view.

Put at its crudest, none of the existing techniques for quantifying the potential effectiveness of individual advertisements ... has provided any relevant or seriously usable data

In looking for the main reasons why such techniques have failed, it is necessary to understand the background against which virtually all of them were developed from the 1940s to the most prolific period of the 1950s and early 1960s. There was a belief then, and many still hold it today, that with adequate resources – human rather than divine – everything is ultimately quantifiable. Further in the practical world it is possible, with enough intelligence to reduce the boundaries of the really relevant areas for measurement of advertising to controllable proportions. Proportions which, although they may not satisfy the academic purist, will provide an adequate, approximate basis for taking the *right* or certainly *better* advertising decisions. In reducing such problems to a manageable scale, a common sense model of how advertising most probably worked was developed.[1] It was a model which the majority of advertising decision-takers accepted then, and which many still do. There were minor modifications in the terms used but such a model was always broadly of this nature:

Advertising stimulus to buyers/potential buyers in product area
(1) Attention.
(2) Brand identification.
(3) Comprehension of copy claim.
(4) Conviction about copy claim.
(5) Action.
Advertising response: normally buying the product

At its simplest there was an advertising stimulus aimed at people who bought products in your product area designed to achieve a response, usually a sale. To be effective the stimulus needed to take your prospects through a number of stages. First to grab his attention, then to make him understand the benefit(s) of your product, to persuade him of the importance of those benefit(s) and thus induce him to buy it.

Techniques for measuring your success at these different stages were developed at various times within the last 30 years or so. Their main need was to be clear, detached and objective and hence expressed in numbers. Interpretation of whether the numbers looked good or bad, were sometimes based on judgment as they stood, by comparison with similar

numbers over time, by comparison with competitors'
numbers, or for the more ambitious by comparison with
norms of varying kinds.

The sorts of measurements which were developed, most
of which are still very much with us here, and even more so
in the States, fell into the main categories listed below:

Stage in stimulus *response process*	*Measurements in numbers*
(1) Attention	Reading/noting score 24-hour/seven-day recall Impact measures
(2) Brand identification	Brand recall
(3) Comprehension of copy claim	Recall of verbal proposition Penetration studies
(4) Conviction	Propensity to buy questions Pre and post attitude shifts Competitive preference shifts
(5) Action	Sales/coupon response

Most of us, I am sure, are very familiar with all the main
techniques above and the, on the whole respectable,
statistical skills involved as well as the often considerable
care and ingenuity in questionnaire formulation.

The main problems that arose in the use of all these
measurements, despite their essentially common-sense
origins, have been that they have produced results which
have been very difficult to reconcile with any reasonable
judgment expectations about particular advertisements and
campaigns. They did not provide common-sense answers.
Anyone trying to cope with them in depth suddenly found

themselves in a nightmare world of apparently purely arbitrary findings. To creative people in particular who were asked to modify their work to make some sense out of such findings, there was just bewilderment and frustration. A frustration which was compounded by an upside-down set of values in which *numeracy* for its own sake was in some unaccountable way equated with *responsibility* and *maturity* and other more self-evident insights were generally disparaged.

But the obvious failure of these measures also prompted a number of people to make what has turned out to be an impressive and internally consistent series of analyses. The main work has been concentrated on repeat purchase consumer goods and has been already extremely well written up and codified notably by Timothy Joyce[2] and Stephen King. On the whole I have found there are very few non-research people in agencies or with advertisers who are particularly familiar with them, which is a pity because some of their findings provide some highly plausible explanations why many of the advertising research measurements in common currency can prove so misleading in their usual application.

Assuming my audience is fully familiar with the details of this work, let me make some highly oversimplified summaries of some of the main conclusions that have been reached.

The first of these refers to those people who are most likely to be receptive to any given advertising. In repeat purchase fields there was extensive evidence of the remarkable stability of purchasing patterns – two or three years after the launch of a new brand you had virtually exhausted your potential new users. Your chances of converting non-users of your brand to use it are then very slim. Your prime need is to intensify the usage of *existing* users. This being so it would explain why advertising research most commonly directed at *total* buyers in a market can produce some highly misleading results *when much of the data is based on the response of people who are not and never will be buyers of your brand.* Again as opposed to communicating with dumb innocents, who approach your advertising in a state of pristine ignorance about your brand, your advertising is primarily concerned with people with past experience of your product, not necessarily thirsting for new knowledge about it. To interpret their response to questions about what they took away from the advertising, it becomes equally important to understand what *they brought to it.*

Second, it was shown that there was a very strong correlation indeed between people's buying behaviour and their attitudes to a brand. Andrew Ehrenberg has shown that given a knowledge of brand penetration you can predict with remarkable accuracy the likely response to most attitude questions. (A relationship perfectly explicable in terms of dissonance theory.) This would explain the irrelevance of so many attitude measurements based on the total market, which often conceal the

In repeat purchase fields there was extensive evidence of the remarkable stability of purchasing patterns – two or three years after the launch of a new brand you had virtually exhausted your potential new users

strength of attitudes among your own buyers, particularly if it is a second or third brand. At the same time there was shown to be an extremely low correlation between recall of advertising and either purchasing behaviour or favourable attitudes. This suggested that the ability to gain high scores in penetration studies from consumers who could parrot your slogans, had no remote connection with advertising effectiveness.

Third, there emerged evidence about the nature of brand personality, which was received as a totality. In the majority of cases such personalities had remarkably little to do with rational, easily verbalised consumer propositions, one of the cornerstones of advertising research. They had much more to do with a complex mixture of past product experience and the moods, symbols and impressions of total brand activity, many aspects of which were not necessarily accessible on semantic differential scales. The more that seems to be learnt about communication, the

There was shown to be an extremely low correlation between recall of advertising and either purchasing behaviour or favourable attitudes

clearer it seems to become that the USA phase of the 1950s, the irrelevant additives and the forced rational claims, were not communicating with consumers in any real sense, but just providing recall fodder for advertising's own introspective 'numbers game'. Whatever recall measurements measured, they provided no solid basis for evaluating advertising.

Finally, there began to be new insights into the nature of 'selective perception' of consumers, who screened out things which had no direct relationship to their purchasing behaviour or interests. Because of this search for consistency, users of a product were more likely to absorb communications about that product which reassured them about their buying behaviour. The exceptionally high reading and noting scores attributed to some early decimalisation advertisements, for example,[3] say much more about the number of people whose behaviour was going to be directly affected, than about the creative excellence of the treatment. Reading and noting scores only have any meaning as numbers, when seen in the context of a mass of other numbers, which it is virtually impossible to make available.

Such findings suggested some clues as to why current measurements were proving largely irrelevant and unusable.

They also suggested a rather different model of the advertising process. Advertising was one important element in the brand personality: effective advertising was often concerned with *consolidating or modifying brand personalities to exert greater influence on the struggle that consumers were facing in reconciling personal beliefs and habits with both their purchasing behaviour and their attitudes to brands.* Although such a struggle sounds rather ponderous and absurd when related to the relatively marginal and trivial nature of brand choice, there is reasonable evidence to suggest that something of this process takes place for however fleeting a moment, at however low a key.

Effective advertising was often concerned with consolidating or modifying brand personalities

It involves the interaction of a mass of variable factors, it involves some factors which are readily quantifiable, *purchasing behaviour* providing the hardest data of all, it also involves even more factors which it would be impractical to quantify on the precise nature of such relationships, which I would certainly submit are by their nature non-quantifiable, but may nonetheless be some of the most important factors of all.

If advertising research is to rely on the measurable and the quantifiable only, it will continue to ask irrelevant questions, and to mislead by ignoring all the big issues which do not lend themselves readily to quantification.

Faced with a model of advertising of this kind, it seems that there are three points of view agencies and advertisers may choose to adopt.

They may say: Advertising is such a complex process that it defies researching, let us therefore rely on the unaided judgment of our creative people. Over recent years there have been agencies who have met some success in this way and some campaigns which have been part of very successful marketing operations have been based on such beliefs. It is an attitude I would find difficult to accept because so much really distinctive creative work is based on pushing back the boundaries of the safe and the predictable with the obvious borderline dangers of irrelevance or shock for its own sake. Uninhibited creativity and self-criticism are mutual contradictions, and one cannot expect creative people to be the soundest critics of their own work.

Or they may say: Everything is capable of quantification, a view that has already been expressed by several speakers, and that the main problems are purely technical ones. In time better techniques will be developed and this is where our main energies should be directed. In the meantime the sort of measurements that we make despite their limitations are better than none. I am afraid this can and often does lead us to make an ambiguous use of present measurements and use them when they seem to prove a point, and suddenly become aware of

We must make the best informed judgment that we can from the most detailed analysis of quantified hard data, but should feel confident in using soft data as well

the shortcomings when they do not seem to fit. It can also lead us, where I believe several people are today, instead of using one unproven and wrong technique to use a whole battery of wrong techniques, as though sheer quantity provides its own validation. I would find this an equally difficult attitude. I share with other less numerate people, like myself, a belief that 'measurements' and 'numbers' are terms which should be used only when we are talking about reasonable degrees of precision.

Also as indicated in the model above, I would suggest a total reliance on the apparently quantifiable prevents us from giving proper attention to the many vital non-quantifiable areas. Or they may say: Creative people need guidance and stimulation from the bravest efforts we can make to understand all those variables we were talking about in that last model of the advertising process. We must make the best informed judgment that we can from the most detailed analysis of quantified hard data, but feel confident in using soft data as well. The fact that the language of insights and impressions gained from group discussions and individual interviews is not necessarily either expressed in numbers or

The emphasis will need to change from systems and techniques ... to the sort of people involved in the creative process and the sort of structure in agencies within which they operate

totally verbalisable should not prevent us from using it to improve our judgments about the validity of advertising.

If you take this last path, and I would hazard that you must be a numerical Spiro Agnew to reject it,[4] it raises some fundamental problems. It means that for a period at any rate (personally I would feel a very long period) the way to make greater progress on providing a better ground for basing decisions on advertising will need to change from systems and techniques, and reducing the statistical error on irrelevant data, to the sort of structure in agencies within which they operate. It has been to cope with this that 'Planning' as the term is used by JWT and ourselves, (and I believe we are the only two agencies, who mean roughly the same thing when we use the term) has been developed.

One of the inevitable consequences of placing value on non-quantifiable data is that an obvious emphasis is put on the people conducting and interpreting the research. Non-quantifiable findings which are reproducible and fill important gaps in our knowledge are as

A personal confrontation with over 2000 instant potato users

valid and significant as the readily quantifiable, but they often require a great deal of intelligence and background understanding to be drawn out. The advertising planner is coming to meet this difficult role and gaining increasing confidence in the process. He has to learn to remain objective, despite the emotional pressures, but this is eased by the independent status he enjoys in the agency, the environment and the open nature of any research undertaken in which clients are always encouraged to participate and frequently do. We have an interesting example of one of our planners who has been on the Smash account for five years.[5] He has personally been involved with some 220 groups and a large number of individual interviews over that time and has had a personal confrontation with over 2000 instant potato users.

He brings to creative development work a depth of knowledge and understanding both of the brand and of how people respond to advertising, which is of far greater practical value than any of the apparently detached typical advertising measurements. It is just this sort of training, trusting and involving able people who develop increasingly better insights by making the best use of information which is quantifiable alongside 'soft' data, which I would suggest is going to provide the most fruitful method of providing a more solid ground for data on which advertising decisions are based in the future. It has all the dangers of putting the emphasis on the calibre of systems. But at a time when the systems are so far removed from solving the real problems they were set up to tackle, and the complexity of such problems makes them so intractable to solution this way, the apparent security of systems and numbers becomes a mirage. With all the obvious problems it poses for the established organisation, the only feasible means of radical improvements lies therefore in some fundamental rethinking of the people we use for advertising research and the environment in which they are able to operate.

This article originally appeared as Pollitt, S. 'Has anything gone wrong with advertising research?' (1971) *Admap*, May.

Notes

How I Started Account Planning in Agencies

1. This situation repeated itself in many US agencies during the 1980s and the recession of the early 1990s, as traditional market research departments were downsized, but not replaced by equivalent scale planning functions. Everywhere the paradox continues – computing power and the 'information explosion' have advanced beyond any expectations, and yet the numbers of staff in advertising agencies specifically responsible for analysing data have declined.

2. In 1979 the notion of 'inclusive' language had hardly become an issue. Stanley and his readers would have understood the masculine gender to include the feminine, and 'account men' could be and often were female.

3. It is worth pointing out that, as at JWT, the original planning department did not represent the addition of extra staff numbers to the agency. In fact at JWT, if anything, it was a rationalisation that slightly reduced numbers, though this was not the object of the exercise.

4. Bob Jones was later media director at BMP, and then went on to found Media Audits. Peter Jones is now chairman of the Tote (the leading British betting organisation). David

Cowan was head of account planning at BMP until 1986 and since then has been a consultant.

5. Some might say that researching rough ads in group discussions became too dominant at one period in BMP – necessarily time-consuming, it shifted emphasis sometimes away from the more strategic uses of research and data. Since 1979 the emphasis has shifted back again, and it is no longer true (as Stanley describes further on) that everything at the agency is subject to this kind of research, nor that planners conduct all their own qualitative research. However, at the time the insistence on researching creative work, and that planners should do this work themselves, were bold and significant moves, and the principles underlying them – getting the ads right, and first-hand consumer contact – remain perennially important. It also emphasised the planner's involvement in the creative execution itself, something that was not universal among subsequent schools of account planning.

6. Stanley's 'now discredited mechanistic techniques' included proposition testing and persuasion testing. He would be surprised to see how widely these are still used today, but I do not think he would have been any more enthusiastic about them.

7. John Webster is still active in creating advertising at BMP DDB Ltd. Over 30 years he has won more creative awards than any other individual in the world.

8. It is worth pointing out that BMP never had higher total staff numbers relative to its income than other agencies, nor did it make an extra charge for account planning

(except in so far as clients normally paid for qualitative research). The size of the planning department was achieved mainly by a correspondingly leaner account management function.

Learning from Research in the 1960s

1. Many would agree that Stanley's fears of 'media research becoming an end in itself' have been borne out by later events, and compounded by the increasing separation of media planning and buying into separate businesses. 'Response functions' – questions of how many times an ad must be seen in order to be effective, and at what point extra exposures become wasteful – are a good example of a real issue that has frequently got lost in narrow academic debate. Recent work by John Philip Jones, Colin McDonald, Simon Broadbent, Erwin Ephron and others has breathed new life into this topic, but one must question how successfully agencies have integrated the learning into their overall planning processes.

2. Colley, Russell (1961) *Defining Advertising Goals for Measured Advertising Results*. New York: ANA. Colley was a management consultant, not really an advertising expert, who applied the 'management by results' theory of the time to advertising. The ANA briefed Colley to address the questions most often asked by advertisers – How much should I spend? Should advertising be a short-term cost or a long-term investment? In fact, the book answers none of these and, rapidly abandoning the attempt to link advertising directly to business results, it takes the easier way out of creating a system of

'intermediate measures' which have dominated much evaluation work ever since. Despite this, *DAGMAR* is not such a bad book as it is often assumed to be – in some ways it was a great leap forward, because it did at least propose evaluating campaigns as a whole in the marketplace instead of merely copy testing individual executions – but its underlying model of advertising effect, the hierarchy referred to here, was naive; and unfortunately this is what *DAGMAR* is mostly remembered for. (One genuine advance in the last 30 years has been an increasing understanding of how to relate advertising to business results through sales modelling and through initiatives such as the IPA Advertising Effectiveness Awards.) *DAGMAR* is still in print.

3. Reeves' theory of 'usage pull' is described in his book, *Reality in Advertising*, published by Alfred A. Knopf in New York, 1960, pp 6–8. Interested readers will have no difficulty in pulling apart the obvious fallacies on which it is based. Nevertheless it was extremely popular and one comes across variations of it even today. *Reality in Advertising* is currently out of print.

4. Haskins, J.B. (1964) 'Factual recall as a measure of advertising effectiveness', *Journal of Advertising Research*, March.

5. Andrew Ehrenberg (now at the South Bank Business School, London) and his colleagues continue to work on patterns of buyer behaviour and to develop the 'reinforcement' theory of advertising. Their most recent publication is a series of reports under the title of 'Justifying our advertising budgets', available from the

South Bank Business School.

6. See Leon Festinger (1957) *A Theory of Cognitive Dissonance*, Stanford, California. The relevance of Festinger's work was to suggest that attitudes were as likely to adapt to behaviour as the other way round, and that people were more likely to accept messages that were consistent with existing beliefs and with their own experience.

7. Stephen King (1965/66) 'How useful is proposition testing?', *Advertising Quarterly Review*, winter (but those who want to follow Stanley's recommendation may not find it easy to trace a copy today).

8. Bill Bernbach was the founder, in 1949, of New York agency Doyle Dane Bernbach, now DDB Worldwide Communications Group. In 1999 *Advertising Age* selected him as the most influential advertising person of the century.

Has Anything Gone Wrong with Advertising Research?

1. This is a version of the 'hierarchical' or 'conversion' model of advertising, originally created by St Elmo Lewis as AIDA (Awareness – Interest – Desire – Action), developed by Daniel Starch in the 1920s, and elaborated by Russell Colley, Lavidge and Steiner, and others in the 1960s. In his original references, Stanley quotes a 1964 article by Kristian S. Palda, 'The hypothesis of an hierarchy of effects'. A more recent and accessible equivalent would be 'A review and critique of the hierarchy of effects in

advertising' by T. Barry and D. Howard, *International Journal of Advertising*, 9(2) 1990.

2. Stanley refers to Timothy Joyce's 1967 paper 'What do we know about how advertising works?' Joyce's paper has been more recently reprinted in *Consumer Behaviour* (ed. Ehrenberg and Pyatt, Penguin 1971), and in *Market Researchers Look at Advertising* (ed. Broadbent, ESOMAR 1980), and really deserves to be made more widely available even today. In 1991 Joyce wrote a sequel to it reviewing what had changed in 25 years ('Models of the Advertising Process' in the ESOMAR Seminar *How Advertising Works and How Promotions Work*, April 1991). Both are worth reading, but on the whole the original paper still stands up remarkably well as an exposition of the system of ideas that Stanley endorses in the present papers. Joyce's 1991 paper is now available under the title 'The advertising process' in a useful compilation edited by John Philip Jones, *How Advertising Works – The Role of Research* (Sage Publications, Thousand Oaks Ca. and London, 1998); this also includes a classic 1974 paper by Andrew Ehrenberg, 'Repetitive advertising and the consumer'. Besides this there is, of course, a huge literature, from which I would particularly recommend Colin McDonald's short book *How Advertising Works, A Review of Current Thinking* (NTC, Henley-on-Thames, 1992) as a general introduction, or John Philip Jones' various books, beginning with *What's in a Name? Advertising and the Concept of Brands* (Lexington Books, Lexington, Mass., 1986). Simon Broadbent's *456 Views of How Advertising Works* (IPA, 1992) contains many useful abstracts and references. Stanley Pollitt, Stephen King and the other architects of account planning placed a lot of

emphasis on understanding how advertising actually works. Do today's planners always give this topic the sustained attention it deserves?

3. In 1971 the UK made the change from shillings and pence to the present decimal currency, which involved an extensive public information campaign.

4. Spiro T. Agnew was vice-president of the USA during Richard Nixon's presidency from 1968 to 1973 (when he resigned following charges of tax evasion and corruption). He was notorious for his eccentric right-wing speeches and often ridiculed as not very intelligent. When asked why he kept Agnew on the ticket in the 1972 election, Nixon replied that: 'No assassin in his right mind would kill me. They know that if they did that they would wind up with Agnew.'

5. Cadbury's Smash was a UK brand of instant mashed potato and one of BMP's first major accounts. The famous Smash 'Martians' campaign is still widely remembered.